50 THINGS TO KNOW
ABOUT BIRDS IN THE USA

If you know someone who loves birds, I cannot imagine them not learning or enjoying this book.

This book is perfect for both experienced birders and beginners alike. It is written in readable prose and studded with personal stories from the author's many years of observing birds.

50 Things to Know About Birds in Pennsylvania: Birding in the Keystone State
Author Darryl & Jackie Speicher

I really enjoyed this book. I live in the Badger state and I learned a lot of things I didn't know before. The author got me excited about taking up bird watching. Definitely going to plan a day trip to Horicon Marsh.

50 Things to Know About Birds in Wisconsin
: Birding in the Badger State
Author Carly Lincoln

50 THINGS TO KNOW ABOUT BIRDS IN FLORIDA

Birding in the Sunshine State

Krystal Hickey

CZYK Publishing Since 2011.
CZYKPublishing.com
50 Things to Know

Lock Haven, PA

ISBN: 9798345729991

50 THINGS TO KNOW ABOUT
BIRDS IN FLORIDA

BOOK DESCRIPTION

Why is Florida one of the best places to see the fall migration of hawks and eagles? Where can I see sandhill cranes in Florida? What is the state bird of Florida? If you find yourself asking any of these questions then this book is for you.

50 Things to Know about the Birds in Florida by Krystal Hickey offers an elegant approach to finding the most beautiful and varied species of birds on the continent. Most books on birding tell you to travel to specific locations and hotspots for one or two prize species on your life list. Although there's nothing wrong with that, this book takes another approach. Here we present you with the regional view of the state, and help you to

locate the habitats and special locations near your travel destination. From this view, we will help you find a diverse community of birds and celebrate the similarities between species. Florida has an extraordinary geography, and there is a great overlap in breeding and wintering ranges for many species. The state is uniquely positioned to offer a variety of habitats with irruptive specialties throughout the year. Based on knowledge from the world's leading experts, understanding the role birds play in their habitat brings a greater appreciation to the art of bird watching.

Florida is unique with having coastline on two different oceans and close proximity to islands. To enhance your birding experience no matter what part of Florida you visit, this book will cover various types of birds and where are the best places to see them.

This book will help you learn which habitats you should visit to find the species you are most interested in, such as water birds, endemic species, and raptors. There are also helpful hints for making some of the more challenging bird identifications. By the time you finish this book, you will know 50 facts about birds and birding in Florida! So grab YOUR copy today. You'll be glad you did.

TABLE OF CONTENTS

6. American Crow

7. Downy Woodpecker

Water Birds

8.Limpkin

9. Anhinga

10. Roseate Spoonbill

11. Purple Gallinule

12. Laughing Gull

13. White Ibis

14. American Flamingo

15. American Coot

16. Reddish Egret

17. Great Blue Heron

18. Black-Crowned Night-Heron

Raptors

19. Swallow-Tailed Kite

20. Snail Kite

21. Bald Eagle

Broward County / Fort Lauderdale
35. Flamingo Gardens

Collier County / Marco Island and Naples
36. Tigertail Beach Park

Palm Beach County
37. Loxahatchee National Wildlife Refuge
38. Juno Dunes and Jupiter Ridge Natural
    Areas

Central Florida
39. Merritt Island National Wildlife Refuge
40. Orlando Wetlands Park

Polk County
41. Lake Kissimmee State Park

53. Honorable Mention:

Other Helpful Resources
50 Things to Know About Birds in the United
States Books

DEDICATION

For Kevin – For always believing in me and pushing me to achieve the next great thing. I am forever grateful for you.

ABOUT THE AUTHOR

Krystal was born in Pennsylvania and moved several times in her early childhood slowly moving south. When she was about 14 she was moved to Daytona, at 16 she was moved to Palm Beach County and was there until 27 when she moved to Pensacola for school. One of the things that she enjoys in her spare time is going on local trails for some exercise and fresh air. While on these walks she would notice birds and that started a beginning interest in birding. Still a beginner, she is interested in visiting more states to witness even more variety of birds.

She is currently still in Pensacola and working on writing more and learning more about birding!

INTRODUCTION

*"A heart without dreams is like
a bird without feathers"*

-Suzy Kassem

Why Florida?

Why come to a state known for beaches and theme parks and go birding? Floridas tropical weather offers beautiful weather nearly all year making it a perfect home for year round birds as well as breeding grounds or migration for birds from colder climates. Florida has over 500 species of birds! Unique habitats such as the Everglades, mangroves and the coasts offer a wide variety of areas for several types of birds, some that are not found anywhere else in the United States.

This book will be a handy guide for the most commonly visited cities in the state and some of the most remarkable and easily identified birds. One must know about the state first so the first tips are going to be some basics on the state and what to expect when visiting. Then we will get into the birds focusing on the most common then moving on to water birds (there is so much water in Florida), then raptors and some honorable mentions that I believe are unique or fun.

The second half of tips will be recommended locations to find these beautiful little birds. The common birds are not always listed at the locations. The main focus is on the rare and/or unique finds in the state. Finally at the end I have included some extra helpful hints for the Florida landscape.

1. ECOSYSTEMS

The amount of variety in the landscape is remarkable considering that Florida is mostly flat. I am going to go over the various ecosystems to help show the diversity that is available.

Florida offers three main types of ecosystems:

Coastal - including mangroves and salt marshes

Mangroves are native to Florida with three different varieties along the coast.

Wetlands - including lakes and rivers

Lake Okeechobee is the largest lake in Florida and one of the largest for the United States.

Upland - including scrub and pine flatwoods

Florida Sand Pine Scrub is endangered

In some areas there are combinations of the above especially in larger parks and forests (yes, Florida does have Forests! Three of them!). There is another specialty of Florida that needs to be explored:

The Everglades (River of Grass)

A wetland covering approximately 200 million acres across Florida, the Everglades is so special. Known to have unique wildlife and plant life it is a main draw to tourism every year. The famous air-boats are what most people associate with the Everglades because of television and they are right! Habitats can include swamps, mangroves and marsh. Approximately 360 bird species can be found here with many of those species being water birds. More information is included in the locations section.

2. REGIONS

Florida is a large state so I decided to break it up into 4 regions that I feel make the most sense for where the different species of birds can be found.

South Florida: This is the southern most point that includes Miami, West Palm Beach and Naples.

Central Florida: Considered to be the heart of the state including Tampa, Orlando, and Daytona Beach.

North Florida: I am considering this in a V shape with Gainesville at the point, then Jacksonville to Tallahassee.

Panhandle: Containing the rest of Florida, Tallahassee to Pensacola.

3. TEMPERATURE

Thousands of vacationers already know that Florida weather is ideal in summer, winter, fall, and spring. Temperatures are mostly consistent throughout the year in much of the state. North Florida and Panhandle are the only places with occasional cold weather. I have even seen Pensacola in recent years get cold enough for snow! Until the sun came out the next day of course, but it did actually snow in Florida. The weather makes Florida a common migratory place for humans and birds alike.

4. FLORIDA'S STATE BIRD

Northern Mocking Bird

Incredible bird that is literally able to mock other bird sounds and songs as well as some human life noises. Some would consider the mockingbird to be aggressive bird with known attacks on family pets and even humans that were too close to nests.

Something unique about mockingbirds is that they are commonly found in developed areas.

Very distinctive plumage make this bird easy to identify and hard to confuse with any other species.

Identification: These birds are medium-sized with small heads and a long tail. The wings are broad and rounded. The length is usually between 8 and 10 inches with the wingspan of approximately 13 inches.

Their coloring is mostly gray-brown with white wing bars on the wings and white outer tail feathers. The beak and feet are black with long legs.

Juveniles can be determined by the spotted

breast

MOST COMMON AND WELL KNOWN SPECIES ACROSS THE UNITED STATES FOUND IN FLORIDA

5. CARDINALS AND BLUE JAYS

These birds are unique in that their colors and wide territory make them instantly identifiable. The male are the more colorful and easiest to spot with bright red and blue colors respectively. These are common Backyard Birds, enjoying the bird feed that homeowners put out to catch these birds. Identification: Both birds are medium sized with the Cardinal being slightly smaller. Male Cardinals are bright red all over and a red beak. Female Cardinals are pale brown with slight red tinges mostly in the wings and tail.

Both genders of the Blue Jays look the same with a blue crest and upper part of the body with a light gray color underneath. Many also feature a black necklace style ring around the neck. They have black eyes, beaks and legs. Blue Jays are pretty distinct however, they could be confused with the Florida Scrub-Jay with the difference being that the Scrub-Jay does not generally have black feathers.

6. AMERICAN CROW

Crows are incredibly intelligent birds that have been observed to make and use tools. The Crow is a common site throughout the United States. The Crow are considered omnivores with a diet consisting of mainly insects and garbage.

Identification: A larger bird with a length between 15-20 inches and a wingspan of 33-39 inches. The Crow has a thick neck and is solid black(legs, eyes, bill, plumage). The wings are rounded and broad with finger-like wingtip feathers.

Most commonly confused with Ravens. One major difference is the size with the Raven being 22-17 inches in length. Ravens are not common in Florida so the comparison shouldn't be necessary while here!

Fun Fact: Crows actually have different sizes based on the region. Crows in Florida are typically smaller with larger feet.

7. DOWNY WOODPECKER

There are several species of woodpecker throughout Florida with this particular breed being the smallest in North America. These are common visitors to backyards with seeds with males more identifiable with the red stripe on his head. Because of their small size, these woodpeckers have been found in walls of buildings!

Identification: These are smaller birds with a length of about 6 inches and a 9-10 inch wingspan. The bird is black and white with stripes on the head and what appears to be checkered wings. As mentioned before the males are identifiable with a red patch on the back of the head.

These can be confused with the Hairy Woodpeckers, they look almost the same. There are two main differences: Hairy Woodpeckers have an obvious longer bill and unmarked outer tail feather compared to the Downy Woodpecker having spotted tail feathers.

8.LIMPKIN

Limpkins are rare birds that are found only in Florida. These birds specialize in eating apple snails with the beak being twisted at the end. This specialization allows them to remove the snail from the shell more easily. They will also eat other aquatic insects, crustaceans and small reptiles/amphibians. There is a rumor that the name Limpkin comes from when they were hunted in Europe where it starts as an apparent limp then into a gallop when being pursued or hunted. The best time to be able to catch a Limpkin is the early morning in marshes.

Identification: This is larger bird with length being 25-28 inches with a wingspan of approximately 41 inches. These birds are mostly a dark brown with white speckling on the neck, back, and wings. The beaks tend to be yellow or brown with dark eyes and brown, long legs. The juveniles look very much like their adults. There are not any species that this bird can get confused for.

They are similar in size to the heron.

Fun Fact: In their taxonomic family,

Aramidae, the Limpkin is the only member!

9. ANHINGA

These birds will always hold a special place for me. Watching this bird dive under the water or airing out their wings is a daily site in Florida and one of my favorites. It is also a fun bird species to say. Anhingas are a common site on any body of shallow water where they dive underneath to hunt their primary food source, fish. After the hunt, they will sit on the edge of the water and stretch out their wings and head high to dry in the Florida sun. This is because the bird does not have waterproof feathers like other water birds. Anhingas can be found all over Florida and the Gulf Coast of the United States, with them moving inland to breed.

Identification: Anhingas are larger birds, almost as large a goose, with a distinctive S-shaped neck and sharp bill. They measure between 29-38 inches with a wingspan around 42 inches. These waterbirds are also good at flying and appear like a cross in the sky with the wings and necks stretched fully while flying.

Male Anhingas are mostly black with some silver or white on the wings and backs. The females and the juveniles look very similar, with a light brown head and neck. Both sexes have yellow bills and feet.

The closest bird that may cause confusion is the Neotropic Cormorant which has a shorter neck and do not have as striking of a wing patch color as the Anhingas.

10. ROSEATE SPOONBILL

Everything about this bird is unique and magnificent. They have a distinctive spoon shaped bill, where their name comes from. These beauties will come to Florida for breeding and has slowly been making homes here. They are only found on the coasts since their main food source is aquatic invertebrates and crustaceans. The preferred habitat is marshlands including wetlands and mangroves. These are the only member of the Spoonbill family to be found in the United States.

Identification: These are large birds that are a unique shade of pink and have long legs. Their lengths can reach 27-34 inches with a wingspan reaching 51 inches. The bill is long and flattened at the end grayish in color. The pink coloration is generally brighter in the shoulders and have red eyes. These are unique birds that may be briefly confused with Flamingos though Flamingos have a longer neck and distinctive bill themselves.

Fun Fact: Roseate Spoonbills will "bald" and lose feathers from the top of their head throughout their adult life! They end up with a light green colored head that make their red eyes more vibrant.

11. PURPLE GALLINULE

These striking water birds can be found in the Southeastern United Stated from Florida to Texas. They live in marshes and prefer to have floating vegetation. They are omnivores that have a preference for hunting invertebrates and frogs. I expected that this would be a threatened species due to its unique coloring however, luckily they are currently low concern for conservation! Identification: The Purple Gallinule is medium sized with an average length of 14 inches and a wingspan of approximately 22 inches. Their bodies and heads are dark purple, iridescent dark green wings (similar to Mallard Duck heads) and back, red and yellow beak and blue fronted — they are not confused with any other species. They have long yellow legs with large, wide feet for staying atop the floating vegetation that they like. Juveniles are pale brown with the hint of the green wings.

12. LAUGHING GULL

These distinct gulls are what indicates it is officially summer. Laughing Gulls are found on the coasts of the east and gulf coast of the United States, breeding in the northeastern coast of the U.S. Their food is generally aquatic invertebrates however, they will also basically beg on the beach and boardwalks for human food.

Identification: Medium sized birds with lengths from 15 to 18 inches and a wingspan from 36 to 47 inches. Laughing Gulls go through several different plumages through their lifetimes. The breeding adult is the most common known colors with a distinct black hood with white arcs above and below the eye and a red beak. When not breeding, the hood disappears and is replaced with a gray colored mask on a mostly white head with a black beak. Juveniles are brown in color with a dark beak. Juveniles do not get adult plumage until about 3 years old.

The Laughing Gull and the Franklin Gull are almost identical. The main difference is that the Franklin Gull has more white on the neck as a juvenile, much larger white spots on the primary feathers as breeding and non-breeding adults.

Fun Fact: When their babies hatch in the nest, the empty eggshell will be removed by the parents. This is because the shell may become lodged in the unhatched egg, where it will not be able to hatch.

13. WHITE IBIS

These are classic sights in Florida wherever there is shallow water. I would see them in the canals after a significant rain in large numbers. They can be found in the southeastern part of the United States from Texas to Virginia. They feed on aquatic invertebrates and insects they find wading in the shallow marshes mostly.

Identification: The White Ibis is medium sized with lengths of 22-26 inches and a wingspan of 26-37 inches. Their beaks are long and curve downward. These birds are almost 100% white except for the black tipped wings. What makes them striking is their red face, beak, and legs. This makes their light eyes very noticeable and distinctive among the wading birds. Juveniles have light brown above and white below and a lighter pink colored bill and legs. As they molt, the brown becomes very splotchy.

The closest possible confusion for the White Ibis is the Great Egret who is also all white.

The Great Egret has a short yellow beak and no red coloration.

Fun Fact: University of Miami uses the White Ibis as a mascot due to the rumored ability to withstand hurricanes (the teams name). Even more fun fact, I am ashamed to admit that as a UM fan I was not aware of this.

14. AMERICAN FLAMINGO

American Flamingos are found in Florida
both wild and in captivity. The wild ones are
believed to be decedents from escaped
ancestors. The American Flamingo is the only
species that is found in North America.
Flamingos use their unique beak to filter the

water through a filter type structure called lamellae.

Identification: These are large birds with lengths of 47-57 inches with a wingspan of 55-65 inches. Flamingos are easily identifiable by their pink plumage (from the diet of crustaceans) and downward facing large beak with a black tip. The wings also have black primary feathers. Juveniles do not have the pink color yet instead are white with black specks or gray color.

15. AMERICAN COOT

These birds (that are not ducks) are
widespread across the United States, Canada,
and Mexico. They live near lakes and ponds.
Although there are attributes of the Coot that
are similar to ducks they are closer related to
cranes and do not have webbed feet. They

also do not waddle when they walk on land. The American Coot is a herbivore feeding on plants near their water homes. It is not common for these birds to take to the sky and fly.

Identification: The American Coot is a good sized bird at approximately 16 inches long and a wingspan of around 23 inches. They have black or dark brown bodies with a very contrasting white bill and forehead and small patch of dark red above the white forehead. Their eyes are red and have yellowish legs. Juveniles have a pale gray under and no white bill or forehead.

16. REDDISH EGRET

Reddish Egrets are found mostly in the Florida Keys and in the Gulf Coast of Texas. These birds are known for their active movements and can be quite a show. They have been witnessed to pace back and forth while flapping their wings and stirring up the water bed with their feet. Their habitat is marshes and they prefer to eat fish.

Identification: They are large birds measuring up to 31 inches long and an average 46 inch wingspan. There are two morphs of this bird. The more common variety is a blue-gray body with muted red neck and head. The other morph is rare and the bird is all white. Both morphs have a shaggy like appearance due to the extended feathers on the head and neck — this is on both morphs. Juveniles of the dark morph are a speckled copper color. This egret could potentially be confused with fellow egrets and herons however the shaggy appearance and flamboyant behavior make this great beauty one of a kind.

17. GREAT BLUE HERON

Another bird that can be found throughout most of the United States are common to see in all parts of Florida. These big birds stalk their prey staying statue still until moving rapidly to catch the fish. They prefer to be in shallow marshes.

Identification: This is the largest bird of the herons in North America with lengths as long as 53 inches and a wingspan of up to 79 inches. The color is blue-gray with a thick black stripe from above the eye to the long crest feathers behind the head. The bill is thick and orange/yellow in color. Juveniles are very similar in color in plumage that matches the bill.

Not many birds can be mistaken for the Great Blue Heron due to the size and coloring. There is a smaller Little Blue Heron that lacks the crown and orange bill.

Fun Fact: Because they have rod receptors in their eyes allowing them to hunt during day and night.

Bonus Fun Fact: They have feathers on their chest that act as cleaner (powder down) to remove oils and fish slimes from the other feathers and beaks! They spread this cleaner to their underparts to protect their feathers from the water.

18. BLACK-CROWNED NIGHT-HERON

Another marshland dweller this little heron feeds on fish and is found in most of North America. These are not the same lanky features of other herons. They are also mostly nocturnal in comparison to their diurnal family. Your best chance to catch this oddity is at dusk as they leave their nests to begin foraging.

Identification: These are mid-range sized for herons with lengths up to 26 inches and wingspans ranging from 25-35 inches. They are considered to be stocky birds with a hunchback look due to tucking their necks in. The coloring looks almost ombre as they have white-light gray under with dark and light gray on their wings and a defined black upper and crown. They have a dark bill with red eyes and light colored legs. Juveniles are brown with white speckling, dark legs, and yellow eyes.

These are pretty unique and not commonly confused with other birds as an adult. As a juvenile other Night-Herons look very similar, with colors being almost identical.

RAPTORS

Predatory Birds are some of the most amazing and exhilarating birds to be able to watch. In Florida there are common occurrences of looking into the sky and seeing a large winged bird gliding through the sky.

19. SWALLOW-TAILED KITE

Florida is one of the few places in the United States that you can catch this raptor. Their diet consists of insects, amphibians, and small reptiles. The best chance of catching a glimpse of this classic raptor is in the summer sky. These birds spend most of their days in flight.

Identification: The key to identification is the deeply forked tail that is very obvious while in the sky. They are on the larger size with being as long as 25 inches and a wingspan of 48 inches. They have a white head and under with black wings, tail and back. They have a curved beach with a hook. Juveniles are a little more fluffy in the head and may not have such a pronounced fork in the tail. Several kites are black and white as well and may be confused for the Swallow-Tailed Kite until it flies. This is the only kite to have such a unique tail. The Magnificent Frigatebird also has a forked tale however, it is a mostly black bird.

Fun Fact: The distinctive tail helps the acrobatics of chasing down flying insects. They will flick their tail to change direction and is able to go backwards.

20. SNAIL KITE

This beautiful endangered raptor is special in that is has a very specific diet. The unique decurved beak helps them with eating their namesake prey of apple snails. The beak allows the bird to remove the snail from the shell for consumption. This diet also limits where they can live. They do best in areas with wetlands making central and south Florida the only place they are found in the United States.

Identification: These are medium-sized for raptors of approximately 16-18 inches with a wingspan ranging from 42-48 inches. The wings are paddle shaped with a square-tipped tail and white base. Males are dark overall with almost black wings and tail, reddish skin around the back and orange feet. Females are lighter in color, more brown is observed and lighter colored feathers around the face. Juveniles look similar to the females with even lighter brown coloration on the head and yellow legs.

Because these birds are distinct shaped, there are not many birds that cause confusion. The closest chance would be a Hook-Billed Kite however, their territories do not overlap.

21. BALD EAGLE

America's Bird can be found in Florida! This distinctive bird has several nesting sites throughout the state with some nests being featured on bird cams that you can login to watch the babies grow. Winter is the best time to see one of these magnificent birds because are more likely to be seen in large numbers and are more widespread especially around water.

Identification: The Bald Eagle is known for their white head and tail with dark bodies. They are large raptors with a length of 27-37 inches and a wingspan of approximately 80 inches. Beaks and feet are the same bright colored yellow. Juveniles are all brown with it taking approximately 5 years to get adult plumage.

FUN FACT: The sound that most movies and TV shows use for the call of the Bald Eagle is not the actual bird. The Bald Eagle has a high pitched sound that is not particularly impressive. Media will use a deeper voiced bird to make the eagle sound more impressive.

22. SHORT-TAILED HAWK

These smaller raptors are only found in Central Florida in the U.S. They hunt smaller birds by flying above them and catching them by surprise.

Identification: Smaller raptors that range in length from 15-17 inches and a wingspan from 32-40 inches. The darker morph is the one that is in Florida with all dark/black body and head with lighter colored wing linings. Their bill is almost black and have yellow legs.

23. OSPREY

This raptor is very common in the United States and all of Florida. They prey of fish and dive from the air to catch them. They are most likely to be found near lakes and ponds year round in Florida.

Identification: Notches in the wings make a distinctive M shape when viewed in the sky.

These are larger raptors with average length of 22 inches and a wingspan ranging from 59-70 inches. The Osprey has a brown upper and stripe on its head with white everywhere else. The feet are white, black beak, and yellow eyes. Juveniles are lighter in coloring and have white spots on the back.

Fun Fact: The success rate of the Ospreys way of fishing can be as high as 70%!

HONORABLE MENTIONS

These are some special birds that you may come across in the great state of Florida.

24. WOOD STORK

The Wood Stork is one of the larger birds on the list and special in how it feeds. The stork drags its feet in the shallow waters and when a fish bumps the beak in the water, the stork reacts and catches the fish. There is a rumor that the reaction time is unparalleled compared to other birds. Luckily for this guy the status of endangerment was down-listed in 2014 to Threatened. Florida is one of the few places that the Wood Stork can be found in the U.S.

Identification: No offense but this is not the best looking bird in the list. The Wood Stork features a fatherless head and some of the neck. They stand almost 3 feet high so they are easy to spot among the egrets and herons wading in the waters. They have a wingspan from 59-68 inches. The Wood Stark is all white except for the under wing feathers and tail which are black. The beak and legs are the same color as the featherless head. Juveniles look very similar however, they have darkish feathers on their heads and necks.

Spoiler Alert: Sadly these big birds do not bring babies. That imagery can be blamed on Hans Christian Anderson who wrote about the White Stork in his fable "The Storks".

25. BURROWING OWL

How fun is it to have an owl that prefers to be in the ground! What makes these little guys even more special is that you are likely to find them in commonly visited areas like sports parks and neighborhood. Florida is the only state on the Eastern United States where these unique owls can be found.

Identification: The long legs are quick identification of the Burrowing Owl if you can find them due to having very good camouflage. They are a little smaller then most owl at a length ranging from 7-9 inches and wingspan of 21 inches. The upper is a brown with white spots and the lower is white with brown spots. They have white "eyebrows" and yellow eyes. Juveniles are less spotted and a little more fluffy.

Fun Fact: Burrowing Owls have an adaptation that allow them to have a higher tolerance for carbon dioxide than any other birds.

26. LONG-BILLED CURLEW

This largest shorebird can be found on the
North-East corner of Florida upwards on the
coast of South Carolina. They prefer
grasslands and prey upon aquatic
invertebrates and insects while on land. The
name is not an exaggeration, the bill of this

bird is insanely long and can be longer than 8 inches.

Identification: Medium sized, the length can be 19-25 inches with a wingspan of 24-35 inches. These gracious birds are a light brown all over with dark speckling from the head to the tail. The neck has some slightly darker streaks. The lower bill is a pink color close to the head with the rest of the bill being black. There may be some confusion with a Whimbrel however, the Whimbrels bill is nowhere near as long or colorful as the Long-Billed Curlew.

Fun Fact: The Long-Billed Curlews unique bill was inspiration for the genus name. Numenius meaning "of the new moon" is a nod to the curvature of the bill resembling the phase of the moon.

27. RED-COCKADED WOODPECKER

What bird list is complete without a woodpecker? The Red-Cockaded

Woodpecker is found throughout the South East of the U.S. They enjoy the pine open woodlands where they make their nests out of the trees. The habitat has been almost depleted so the best chance to see this lovely is to visit a preserve or national park with pines. They have been listed as Endangered since 1970 due to the habitat shrinkage.

Identification: Smallish woodpecker with an average length of 8 inches and a wingspan of 14 inches. They have large white cheeks that contrast against the spotted black and white wings. The males have the name sake red-cockade, a red stripe that is on the cheek. Even though the red is the namesake, it can be difficult to see.

Ironically the other woodpeckers that could be confused with the Red-Cockaded Woodpecker have obvious red spots or stripes. This includes the Downy Woodpecker (back of the crown), Hairy Woodpecker (same location and more of an orange color) and the Yellow-Bellied Sapsucker (crest and throat).

Fun Fact: Cockade is in relation to hats! It is the ornament (usually a ribbon) worn on a hat.

28. PAINTED BUNTING

These vivid songbirds can be found throughout the South from Texas to South Carolina. This brightly colored bird can become a backyard bird due to a diet of seeds and prefer dense vegetation. You can find these on trails if you are patient. Identification: These small songbirds are usually about 5 inches long. They have a typical seed bill that is stubby and black in color. Males are the more vibrant of the sexes with bright blue head, bright light green wings, and bright orange chest, back, and tail. Females are a vibrant green and still remarkable. Juveniles are also mostly the same green color as females with juvenile males having darker chests.

29. FLORIDA SCRUB JAY

This bird is only found in Florida due to the habitat of the Sand Scrub and are very rare. There is an estimated fewer than 8,000 remaining in the world. The Florida Scrub Jay is genetically different from the other members of the scrub family making them

Floridas very own. They tend to be very curious and have been known to become hand-tame in places with frequent human contact. They are found in the central part of the state like a thick band coast to coast.

Identification: This is an average sized jay with length averaging 10 inches and wingspan of 13-14 inches. They are blue with lighter belly, back, forehead, and throat. They have black eyes, beak and feet. Juveniles have more gray and do not have the blue head.

Other Scrub-Jays have very similar coloring and could easily be mistaken for the Florida Scrub-Jay. There are two definitive ways to determine the Florida Scrub-Jay from the others: the Florida Scrub-Jay has the lighter forehead unlike any of the others and none of the territories overlap. If you are in Florida, it can only be our own Scrub-Jay.

Fun Fact: Due to the Florida Scrub Jay not being able to be dispersed due to their habitat, the three main populations in central, southwestern and northern all have distinct vocalizations!

30. BLACK NODDY

Originally found in 1960 in the Florida Keys this beautiful bird calls the tropical islands home, coming to the Florida Keys to possibly nest. They like to feed on small aquatic lifeforms such as fish, shrimp and krill. Identification: These smaller birds have a length of approximately 13 inches and a 30 inch wingspan. The Black Noddy is almost entirely black (including legs, bill, and eyes) except the head and neck. They have a white forehead that shifts into a grey neck then black back.

Easily confused with the Brown Noddy, the Black Noddy is a smaller, darker colored bird with a longer bill.

31. WHERE CAN YOU FIND THESE BEAUTIFUL BIRDS?

Florida offers a Great Florida Birding Trail with more than 500 sites across the state for premier birding. Some of these locations will be listed, but please check out the website for more sites! I am going to be providing some of the best places based off of the regions as above: South Florida, Central Florida, North Florida, and Panhandle. I will be focusing on the bigger cities for the most part with some honorable mentions.

- South Florida:
- Florida Keys
- Dry Tortugas

Located at the end of the Florida Keys and consisting of 7 islands, Dry Tortugas National Park is the furthermost spot to do some birding. Due to being closer to South America they have more birds than I mentioned above including the Peregrine Falcon and Frigatebirds to name a few. This is also where the Black Noddy was found.

The location of the park offers varied bird species throughout all seasons making this a lovely trip year round! The website offers a downloadable map to better plan your birding. They even have a museum for when the birding is done!

32. MIAMI

Cutler Wetlands - Nature Preserve
This is not like the other locations listed, this is a nature preserve that is surrounded by neighborhoods. I recommend this location due to the variety of birds that you may be able to catch. There are reports of common birds like the Cardinal and Blue Jay, raptors like the Bald Eagle and Short-Tailed Hawk, as well as water birds like the Laughing Gull

and Anhinga. There is also a good chance that you can catch the state bird as well! This location is not one that offers trails or that you may want to stay all day however, there is the possibility of seeing a Wood Stork or Osprey!

33. BISCAYNE NATIONAL PARK

This national park is a treasure for bird watching offering several birding trails. These trails vary in location, length, and time. Some of the trails are better accessed with paddle boards or kayaks due to the park being very rich with water. Birds you may catch from our list is the White Ibis, Great Blue

Heron with other varieties including Mangrove Cuckoos (largest population in Florida) and Brown Pelicans. Biscayne National Park also offers a variety of other outdoor activities like fishing, boating, diving, and guided tours. There is a visitor center, gallery and museum as well if the weather is not cooperating. There is so much to do, I would consider it a must do if in Miami!

34. EVERGLADES NATIONAL PARK

When you think of visiting Florida there are two things that come to mind - Disney World and the Everglades. The Everglades are Americas largest subtropical wilderness this means that there are several rare and endangered species that call the Everglades home. There are more than 300 species of birds that have been seen here. Birds you will likely catch are Wood Storks, White Ibis, Great Blue Heron, and Roseate Spoonbill. The website offers resources on the best places to catch sightings of particular birds or what you may find based off of where you plan on visiting and a list of the endangered and threatened birds. The Everglades are a unique experience that should be done if possible — highly recommended by local Floridians!

35. FLAMINGO GARDENS

As the name suggests Flamingos are one the main species available to be seen here. They offer a wildlife sanctuary that includes an aviary with over 200 species of birds that are not able to be released back to the wild. They also have an aviary dedicated to parrots that have also been rescued. There is a pond on the property where Flamingos roam free (and the children can feed). The wildlife sanctuary also offers other animals to visit including crocodiles, otters, panthers, and black bears!

There are rumors that you may be able to catch some wild birds including Swallow-Tailed Kite in the summer and Limpkins near the pond. If you are lucky you may also be able to catch a Painted Bunting or two in the winter! Flamingo Gardens also offer a botanical gardens and museum on the property for a full day of adventures.

36. TIGERTAIL BEACH PARK

Approximately a half hour from Naples is Tigertail Beach. Consisting of white sands and a birding tower that was added to the park in 2016 at this park you have the chance to catch some great species of birds. Snowy Plover can be found as well as Reddish Egrets and Bald Eagles. Depending on the season you may be able to catch the Long-Billed Curlew. Around on the island you may also be able to find some Burrowing Owls! Due to this little beach being formed from a hurricane this beach is considered a "barrier island in the making" with the beach also being known for shelling (seashells that are found along the beach) and a tidal lagoon. Reportedly this little gem is not as well known as some of the other locations on the list so it may not be overly populated. They also offer picnic areas and playgrounds making it a great place to take the whole family for a day in the sun!

PALM BEACH COUNTY

I lived in Palm Beach County for several years so some of my suggestions may be a bit biased.

37. LOXAHATCHEE NATIONAL WILDLIFE REFUGE

On this northern end of Everglades there are over 250 species that available for birding throughout the year. This is one of the places you may be able to catch the endangered Snail Kite. Other birds include Osprey, Bald Eagles, Painted Buntings, Limpkins, Anhingas and Wood Storks. The website offers a Bird Checklist that includes all the birds that you are likely to see while visiting. The main focus of this refuge is trails for walking and wildlife watching however, they also offer fishing, boating, and hunting depending on the time of year. This refuge also allows pets to be taken in designated parts of the trails. Finally there is a visitor center and a butterfly garden that offers education on the area.

38. JUNO DUNES AND JUPITER RIDGE NATURAL AREAS

These natural areas are approximately 2 miles apart and I have included them for one large reason: This is a location where the rare

Florida Scrub-Jay can be found! Both locations are also part of the Great Florida Birding Trail with the Juno Dunes boasting the highest natural point in Palm Beach County. Both are along US-1 which is a great alternative to Interstate 95 along the East coast.

Juno Dunes also offers multiple trails and observation tower.

Jupiter Ridge has the additional chance to see a manatee swim by! There are also trails and observation platform as well as canoe or kayak access.

For an additional Florida experience, I recommend going across the street to Loggerhead Marinelife Center. This is a turtle hospital that has turtles that have been rescued from around the area and then released once they are healed.

CENTRAL FLORIDA

Starting in the most central city of the state: Orlando

39. MERRITT ISLAND NATIONAL WILDLIFE REFUGE

Originally founded as protection for migratory birds this refuge is well-known to be a lovely birding spot boasting more than 350 species. Originally this land was bought for use by NASA for the John F. Kennedy

Space Center. Since not all the land was needed for the center this refuge was set aside for protection in 1963. Some of the birds commonly seen include Bald Eagles, Reddish Egrets and Roseate Spoonbills. Merritt Island Wildlife Refuge is also home to one of the larger populations of the Florida Scrub-Jay. There is a visitor center and a car tour for wildlife viewing. As with most refuges fishing, hiking and hunting are other available activities.

Fun Fact: The website offers a PDF bird list to print off to check off as you see the possible birds!

40. ORLANDO WETLANDS PARK

This is a manmade wetland that has grown to have over 150 permanent species with over 200 spotted over the years. Some common birds are Black-Crowned Night-Herons and American Coot with uncommon sightings of the Short-Tailed Hawk and Swallow-Tailed Kite. This park is an open space walking and observation area. This park does not allow boating, fishing or hunting although they do offer grills and picnic tables for a little lunch while birding! Their website also offers a brochure style bird checklist that details the seasons and likelihood of catching the birds that visit. The website also offers checklists for butterflies, dragonflies, and fauna & flora.

41. LAKE KISSIMMEE STATE PARK

This state park has a little bit of everything to offer. They have many trails for walking/hiking with some of them available for equestrians, picnic area and pavilions, campsites, boating, fishing, and canoeing/kayaking. Lake Kissimmee State Park is surrounded by 3 lakes: Lake Kissimmee (the largest to the East), Lake Rosalie, and Tiger Lake. Over 150 species have been observed with some of the most common birds including Eastern Whippoorwill, Little Blue Heron, Barn

Swallow, Cooper's Hawk, and Short-Tailed Hawk.

TAMPA AREA

42. COCKROACH BAY AQUATIC PRESERVE

This was named for Horseshoe Crabs, not the cockroach insect so if you are anything like me you can sigh in relief. This preserve is one of the most pristine in the area due to be minimally developed. This site is more of a walking/birding trail than tourist attraction. The preserve has had over 250 species spotted, with over 20 species of just ducks especially in the winter. Other species include

Reddish Egrets and Gray Kingbirds. This is also included in the Great Florida Birding Trails.

43. LETTUCE LAKE PARK

One of the most popular parks in the Tampa area, this park offers wonderful birding as well as hiking and canoeing/kayaking. Most of the park is a floodplain of Hillsborough River and hardwood swamp forest. There is a paved trail and boardwalk, and observation tower for a view of the Hillsborough River. Some birds you may be able to catch are Barred Owl, Osprey, Sandhill Cranes and Canadian Geese. There are birdwatching tours offered a few times a month with a couple through the Tampa Audubon Society (these ones need to be registered for). There is also a playground for the children and some picnic areas.

DAYTONA / VOLUSIA COUNTY

44. LYONIA PRESERVE

The main focus of the Lyonia Preserve is to offer education and to restore the Florida scrubs. The main habitant of the scrubs are the Florida Scrub Jay (which is also the mascot of the preserve) and they offer tours to get up close and personal to these threatened birds. The preserve offers three hiking trails of various lengths. Other birds that you may be able to see include Great Blue Herons, Whippoorwills, Northern Mockingbird, and Downy Woodpeckers. There is also an environmental center that offers education on the scrubs and local wildlife.

MARION COUNTY

45. OCALA NATIONAL FOREST

Florida has three national forests with this one located between Orlando and Gainesville. There are over 600 water features and is a great place for birding and wildlife viewing.

The forest itself is approximately 383,000 acres and offers everything needed for an adventurous vacation. They offer fishing, boating, hunting and camping throughout the forest. Luckily there is a trail inside the park that is fantastic for birding, the Salt Springs. There is a trail and an observation deck to get the most out of this wildlife viewing area. Birds that live here include the Florida Scrub Jay, Ovenbird, Limpkin, Green Heron, and Red-Cockaded Woodpecker. Salt Springs offer full hookups for RVs and you can rent canoes to paddle the Salt Springs Run.

46. JACKSONVILLE AREA

Timucuan Preserve

This national preserve is over 46,000 acres consisting mostly of wetlands. This preserve is split up into separate parks with the best one for birding being the Theodore Roosevelt Area. The Willie Browne Trail ends in a bird observation platform overlooking the marsh. You are likely to see Bald Eagles. Vultures, Swallow-Tailed Kite, common ducks, Laughing Gull, and Sandhill Crane. This preserve is special in that there is a fort (Fort Caroline) and a plantation (Kingsley

Plantation) also included. Some other activities you can do that is a scenic drive, hiking, visit an archaeological site, fish, and visit the museum.

47. GAINESVILLE AREA

Lochloosa Wildlife Conservation Area
Another trail on the Great Florida Birding and Wildlife Trail, this area consists of more than 11,000 acres and is designed to help with species diversity. Large quantities of Bald Eagles call this preserve their home. Other species you may come across are Barn Swallows, Barred Owl, Purple Gallinule, Cattle Egret, and Red-Winged Blackbird. Other activities available are hunting, fishing,

and boating. Horseback riding is allowed if you have horses!

48. ICHETUCKNEE SPRINGS STATE PARK

About an hour north of Gainesville, Ichetucknee Springs is a National Natural Landmark with its pristine, crystal clear waters. The state park includes the Ichetucknee River, Grassy Hole Spring and Blue Hole Spring along with the namesake. For this park, there is no set bird-watching spot however, there are three hiking trails that offer different lengths and environments. Some species that you should see are Wood

Duck, Swallow-Tailed Kite, Wild Turkey, American Kestrel and Red-Tailed Hawk. With all the beautiful waterways another way to bird watch is to tube down the 6-mile river. Other activities available include scuba diving, paddling (kayaks/canoes/paddle boards), playground, and picnicking. They even offer to have weddings in the park!

49. PANHANDLE

Tallahassee Area

Alfred B. Maclay Gardens State Park

This is one of my favorite places in Florida. If you are on social media and want incredible photos, this is the place. The garden is absolutely magnificent and due to all the flowering plants many species of bird are attracted to the area. Besides the garden itself there are also several trails and a place to fish or do some paddling on Lake Overstreet. Some of the more common birds seen in this park are the Green Heron, Ruby-Throated Hummingbird, Cooper's Hawk, Barred Owl, Wood Stork, and Belted Kingfisher. For the full garden experience the best time to visit is January through the end of April.

50. EDWARD BALL WAKULLA SPRINGS STATE PARK

This spring is the one that is pictured when someone says Florida spring. This spring is the deepest and largest in the world. What makes this spring even more special is the fact that is it surrounded by a cypress swamp that is rumored to be ancient. It has even been the scene for two movies! This is a very special place that should be visited if you have the opportunity. Just about every outdoor activity is available including biking, hiking, boat tours (very highly recommended for birding), snorkeling/scuba diving, and events. Other wildlife is also abundant including manatees, alligators, and turtles. There are over 200 hundred species observed in the park. Some of the most commonly seen have been Louisiana Waterthrush, Broad-Winged Hawk, Tricolored Heron, Great Horned Owl and Eastern Screech-Owl.

51. PENSACOLA AREA

University of West Florida: Edward Ball Nature Trail

Keeping with the Edward Ball theme, this is a great little trail on the University of West Florida campus. It is only about a half mile long but you can catch quite the variety of birds. Common to catch on this trail are American Bittern, Downy Woodpecker, Red-Eyed Vireo, and Eastern Screech Owl. Every time I have gone, there has been alligators and turtles too!

52. GULF ISLANDS NATIONAL SEASHORE: FORT PICKENS

Gulf Islands National Seashore is the longest seashore that is protected federally in the U.S. It starts in spans two counties and has 5 different beaches. Fort Pickens is the westernmost of Pensacola Beach and has the most varied birding of the 5 locations with over 300 species being observed. One of the species seen here is the Painted Bunting, one of the most vibrant birds in Florida. Other common birds that can be seen are Hooded Oriole, Acadian Flycatcher, Mississippi Kite, and Osprey. Since it is a beach you can also boat, fish, snorkel and camp in the park as well. I feel I should also tell you that the beaches are breathtaking with white sands and clear water.

53. HONORABLE MENTION:

As I mentioned before, I lived in Palm Beach County for some time and one of my favorite places to go was:

Grassy Waters Nature Preserve

It is a little bit of a drive to get here but I feel the wildlife and birding is worth it. This preserve is mostly for walking and observing wildlife with no real frills. There is a visitor center with a small little museum that educates about the area and how to preserve it. The most common birds are the Great Blue

Heron, Eurasian Collared-Dove, Loggerhead Shrike, Northern Mockingbird and the Tree Swallow. You may also be able to find a Snail Kite, Swallow-Tailed Kite, and Limpkin.

BONUS TIPS:

Hurricanes

- If there is a hurricane expected in your area, please be sure to stock up on essentials such as   water and non-perishables and take shelter.

- Do not always listen to locals. We have been through many storms and sometimes can forget that they are serious and scary. Plus dark humor is how Florida functions.

- Due to previous storms that have happened, please always verify the above locations are fully operational before heading out. Depending on the damage some parks may have parts or the whole park shut down.

Weather

- For most the year it is HOT in Florida. There are no such things as seasons especially in South Florida. North Florida and the Panhandle do have winters that get a bit chilly in November - February. Then it goes right back to HOT. Please keep this in mind when you are in the parks. Make sure to bring sunscreen, water, and maybe a hat before heading out into the Florida sun.

- Humidity is the killer. What they say is true, it is a wet heat. Sometimes you will leave the air conditioning and feel the heat sit on you.

- Rain is not terribly predictable. When it does rain, wait and it will go away. Return to the above humidity.

- Florida weather is absolutely magnificent. This really is a haven for all outdoor activities, as long as you are prepared. Please be safe.

Pets

- If you are traveling with your pets, please be sure to check the individual trail for pet allowance. Some trails may allow leased pets on certain trails while others do not allow pets at all.

- Please do not leave your animal in the car with no air conditioning. As mentioned above it is HOT in Florida and it very easy for the animal to become overheated.

OTHER HELPFUL RESOURCES

Audubon Guide to North American Birds: A great resource from the premier bird advocacy group, the Audubon Society. https://www.audubon.org/bird-guide

Bird Watching Daily: This site is specifically built to help you find hotspots anywhere. This link you can use for Florida specifically.

eBird: Online birding database with information based off of location and even has "Hotspots" with high variety of birds.

Florida Birding Trail: This is the website where you can find many of the trails listed above and more.

https://www.birdwatchingdaily.com/hotspots/locations/florida/

https://www.ebird.org

https://www.floridabirdingtrail.com

The Cornell lab of Ornithology: This is an excellent resource for all things birds from Cornell University. Their app can help identify birds sounds.

https://www.birds.cornell.edu/ eBird

https://ebird.org/home An online database of bird observations providing scientists, researchers and amateur naturalists with

real-time data about bird distribution and
abundance.

The National Audubon Society. The National
Audubon Society protects birds and the
places they need, today and tomorrow,
throughout the Americas using science,
advocacy, education, and on-the-ground
conservation. https://www.audubon.org/

U.S. Fish and Wildlife Services Birds of
Conservation Concern
https://www.fws.gov/birds/management/
managed-species/birds-of-conservation-
concern.php

READ OTHER
50 THINGS TO KNOW ABOUT BIRDS
IN THE UNITED STATES BOOKS

Stay up to date with new releases on Amazon: https://amzn.to/2VPNGr7

CZYKPublishing.com